Little Women

Sept 05

RETOLD BY PAULINE FRANCIS 4·0

D0434627

Evans

EVANS BROTHERS LIMITED

Published by Evans Brothers Limited
2A Portman Mansions
Chiltern Street
London W1U 6NR

© Evans Brothers Limited 2003
First published 2003

Printed in Hong Kong

British Library Cataloguing in Publication data
Francis, Pauline
    Little Women
    1. March family (Ficticious character) - Juvenile fiction
    2. United States - Social life and customs - Juvenile fiction 3.
    Children's stories
    I. Title II. Alcott, Louise M. (Louisa May), 1832 - 1888

ISBN 023752533X

Introduction

Louisa May Alcott was born in Philadelphia, America, in 1832. She is best remembered for *Little Women*, which was published in 1868. It was the first children's book in America to become a classic.

Louisa was the second of four daughters. When she was young, the Alcott family lost a great deal of money. So as soon as she was old enough, Louisa helped her family by running a small school, taking in sewing and becoming a tutor to an invalid girl. Later, she wrote horror stories for magazines and newspapers. Then she began to write stories for girls.

Little Women was the first of these stories and it was very successful. The second part, known as *Good Wives*, was published a year later. *Little Women* tells the story of the March girls – Meg, Jo, Beth and Amy – during the American Civil War. This war was fought between the Northern states of America (where the March family lived) and the Southern states, from 1861 to 1865. The story tells us little of the war itself, but it describes the ups and downs of the family's life. It is a moral story – it tells the reader clearly what is right and wrong.

Louisa May Alcott wrote other books about the March girls when they were grown up. She died in 1888.

CHAPTER ONE

A merry Christmas

"Christmas won't be Christmas without any presents," Jo grumbled.

"I don't like being poor," Meg sighed, looking down at her old dress. "I wish father hadn't lost all his money. Then I wouldn't have to teach those dreadful children every day."

"You don't have to spend all day with bad-tempered old Aunt March!" Jo said. "She has me running after her all day long."

"I don't think it's fair for some girls to have pretty things, and other girls nothing at all," Amy complained. "The girls at school laugh at my dresses."

"We've got father and mother and each other," their sister Beth said quietly.

"We haven't got father," Jo said sadly. "And he will be away for as long as the war lasts."

The four sisters sat knitting while the snow fell softly outside. Margaret, the eldest, was sixteen. She was plump and fair-haired and very pretty. She was proud of her hands, which were soft and white.

Jo, one year younger than Meg, was very tall, thin and brown. She had a determined look on her face and sharp grey eyes. Jo's long thick hair was her one beauty but she usually kept it pinned up out of the way. Her hands and feet were big and she looked like somebody who was growing too fast and didn't like it.

Elizabeth – or Beth as everybody called her – was a bright-eyed girl of thirteen. She was shy and always peaceful. She seemed to live in a happy world of her own. Amy was the youngest of the four. She was very beautiful, pale and slim. Her yellow hair curled over her shoulders and her eyes were blue.

The clock struck six and Beth put a pair of slippers to warm by the fire. Meg lit the lamp. Amy got out of the armchair without being asked, and Jo held the slippers closer to the fire to warm. Their mother, Mrs March, would be home soon.

Later, as they gathered around the table to eat, Mrs March patted her pocket.

"I've got a treat for you after supper," she smiled.

"A letter!" Jo cried. "A letter from father!"

"Yes, and a nice long one," her mother said.

As soon as they had finished eating, Mrs March took out the letter and read it to her daughters: "…Give the girls all my love and a kiss," she finished. "Tell them I think of them every day and night. I know they will be loving children and do their duty so that, when I come home, I may be even prouder of my little women."

"When will he come home, marmee?" Beth whispered.

"Not for many months, dear," her mother replied. "The soldiers need him more than we do."

Jo was the first to wake up on Christmas morning. No stockings hung at the fireplace. But their mother had given each of them a book and the girls read quietly. When they went downstairs, Hannah, who had lived with the family since Meg was a baby, was in the kitchen.

"Where is mother?" Meg asked.

"Goodness only knows," Hannah sighed, her face worried. "A young boy came begging at the door early this morning and your ma went back with him to see what was needed."

They waited at the table for more than an hour, eager for breakfast. At last, the front door banged.

"Merry Christmas, mother," the girls shouted. "Thank you for our books. We shall read them every day!"

"Merry Christmas, little daughters," Mrs March called. "Now listen. Not far from here lies a poor woman with a newborn baby. Six other children are huddled in one bed to keep warm. My girls, will you give them your breakfast as a Christmas present?"

At first, nobody spoke. Then Meg fetched a basket and they all put in the food from the table. That was a very happy breakfast, though they didn't get any of it.

On New Year's Eve, Meg and Jo went to a party.

"Now what shall we wear?" Meg asked her sister.

"What's the point of asking?" Jo muttered. "You know we shall wear our old cotton dresses because we haven't got anything else."

"If only I had a silk dress," Meg sighed.

When the time came for their sisters to get ready, Beth and Amy pretended to be maids. There was a great deal of running up and down, laughing and talking. Then, suddenly, a strong smell of burning filled the house.

"Should the curling tongs on Meg's hair smoke like that?" Beth asked.

"It's the dampness drying," Jo replied. "You'll see, Meg will have a beautiful row of ringlets across her forehead when I take off the tongs."

Jo removed the tongs, but no cloud of ringlets appeared. Instead, Meg's hair came with them.

"What have you done?" Meg wept. "Oh, my hair! I can't go to the party! I can't." But she did go, and she and Jo looked very pretty in their simple dresses.

"If you see me doing anything wrong, just remind me with a wink, will you?" Jo asked.

"No, winking isn't lady-like," Meg told her. "I'll lift my eyebrows instead."

At the party, Jo felt out of place. When the dancing began, she saw a red-headed youth coming towards her and hid behind a curtain. Unfortunately, another shy person was already there. Jo came face to face with a boy.

"Stay if you like," the boy laughed. "I only came here because I don't know many people."

"So did I," Jo said politely. She stared at him.

"I think I have had the pleasure of meeting you before," she said even more politely. "You live near us, don't you?"

"Next door," he replied. There was a long silence.

"How is your cat, Miss March?" he asked at last.

"Well, thank you, Mr Laurence," she replied. "But I am not Miss March, I'm only Jo."

"And I'm not Mr Laurence. I'm Laurie," he laughed.

"Laurie Laurence," Jo said. "What an odd name!"

"My first name is Theodore, but I don't like it," Laurie told her. "The boys try to call me Dora, so I make them say Laurie instead."

As they talked like old friends, Jo took several good looks at the Laurence boy. Curly black hair, brown skin, big black eyes, handsome nose, fine teeth, small hands and feet, and taller than her! How Jo enjoyed the rest of the evening! And how sorry she was when it ended!

"I don't believe rich young ladies enjoy themselves any more than we do," she whispered to Meg as they went to bed, "in spite of our burnt hair and old gowns."

And I think she was right.

CHAPTER TWO
Neighbours

Jo glanced across to the Laurence house as she swept snow from the garden path. It was a fine house, made of stone with beautiful curtains at every window. But it was a lonely house.

"That boy needs the company of young people," she told her sisters.

She looked up from the garden and saw Laurie's curly head at the window. She picked up a handful of snow and threw it at the glass. Laurie opened the window.

"Are you ill?" Jo called.

"I've had a bad cold," he told her. "It's as dull as a grave up here."

"Don't you read?" she asked in surprise.

"Not much," Laurie replied.

"Why doesn't somebody come and see you?" Jo asked.

"Boys make such a noise and my head hurts," he replied. He paused. "Will you come?"

"I'm not quiet," Jo said, "but I'll come."

Laurie and Jo talked for a long time. Jo was surprised to learn that Laurie already knew a lot about the March family.

"When I'm alone up here, I can't help looking over at your house," he explained. "Sometimes, when the lamps are lit and you forget to draw the curtains, I watch you all around the table with your mother." Laurie's voice trembled. "I haven't got a mother, you know."

The lonely look on Laurie's face went straight to Jo's warm heart. "We'll never draw the curtains again," she said, her sharp voice gentle. "But, instead of peeping at us, I want you to come over and see us."

They started to talk about books.

"If you like books so much, let me show you our library," Laurie said. "Grandpa is out so you needn't be afraid."

"I'm not afraid of anything!" Jo said, tossing her head.

Just then the doctor called to see Laurie, so Jo found herself in the library on her own. She stood for a moment in front of a portrait of Laurie's grandfather.

"I might be afraid of him," she said out loud, "his mouth is severe, and he looks as if he is strong-willed. He isn't as handsome as my grandfather, but I like him."

"Thank you, ma'am," a gruff voice said behind her. And there, to Jo's dismay, stood old Mr Laurence.

Poor Jo blushed until she couldn't blush any redder, and her heart began to beat very fast. For a minute, she wanted to run away – but that was cowardly and the others would laugh at her.

"So you are afraid of me, hey?" the old man asked.

"Not much, sir."

"But you like me in spite of it?"

"Yes, I do, sir."

The answer pleased the old gentleman. He laughed and shook Jo's hand.

"So you think Laurie needs cheering up?" he asked.

"Yes, sir," Jo replied. "He seems lonely."

When they had tea, Mr Laurence saw the change in his grandson. He had colour and life in his face. But when Laurie began to play the piano, Jo noticed the sad look that came across the old man's face. That evening, at home, her mother explained.

"Laurie's father ran away and married an Italian lady," she said. "She was a musician. Laurie's grandfather did not approve of the marriage. But both parents died and Laurie's grandfather took him in. The music reminds him of that unhappy time."

"How romantic!" Meg exclaimed.

"How silly!" Jo said. "He should let Laurie be a musician if he wants, not force him to go to college."

The big house next door became an enchanted palace for the March girls. Nobody was afraid of Mr Laurence, except timid Beth. What good times they had! Sleigh-rides, skating and little parties at the big house, Meg walking in the conservatory full of flowers, Jo reading, Amy copying pictures. Only Beth, who longed to see the grand piano, could not pluck up the courage to go. She went once, with Jo, but old Mr Laurence did not realise how shy she was. He spoke so loudly that she was afraid to go again. Fortunately, the old man got to hear about it. He called at the March house and said to Mrs March.

"Laurie neglects his music now, and I'm glad. He was getting too fond of it. But the piano needs playing. Would some of your girls come and practise, now and then, just to keep it in tune?"

Beth took a step forward. Mr Laurence went on quietly. "They needn't see or speak to anyone."

Beth spoke at last.

"I'm Beth," she whispered, "and I'll come if you are quite sure nobody will hear me."

After that, Beth slipped through the hedge every day and played the piano. She never knew that Mr Laurence often opened his study door to listen to her tunes.

Beth made a pair of slippers for Mr Laurence to thank him. She sent them to him with a short note. A day passed and Beth did not hear back from Mr Laurence. Had she offended him? On the second day, Beth took her dolls out for a walk. When she came back, she saw her sisters watching for her at the window.

"Oh, Beth, he's…"Jo began, but Meg slammed down the window.

They dragged Beth into the parlour. She stared, pale with surprise. There, in front of her, stood a small piano.

"For me?" Beth gasped, holding on to Jo so that she would not fall over. At last, Beth sat down to play.

"You'll have to go and thank him," Jo said, as a joke.

Nobody thought Beth could really do that. But to the amazement of the whole family, Beth walked down the garden, through the hedge, and into the Laurence's house. They would have been even more amazed if they had seen what happened next. Beth went to the old gentleman's study door, knocked, went in and started to say 'thank you'. But she didn't finish. Instead she put both arms around Mr Laurence's neck and kissed him.

CHAPTER THREE

Amy gets into trouble!

One day, as Laurie rode by on his horse, Amy sighed.

"I just wish I had a little of the money Laurie spends on that animal," she muttered.

"Why?" Meg asked kindly.

"I need it so much. I'm in dreadful debt."

"In debt, Amy? What do you mean?" Meg asked, her voice more serious.

"It's the fashion to eat pickled limes," Amy explained. "Everybody's taking them to school, although they're not allowed. I owe at least a dozen. If one girl likes another, she gives her a lime. I've taken ever so many, and I've got to start giving them."

Meg opened her purse and took out a dollar coin.

"Make this last as long as you can," she said.

The next day, Amy was rather late to school. When she arrived, she was clutching a brown paper parcel, which she put in her desk. A rumour soon started. Amy March had twenty-four delicious limes. The attention from her friends was overwhelming. One girl invited Amy to a party, another helped her with her sums, yet another lent her a watch until playtime. But one girl was jealous and she told the teacher, Mr Davis.

"Miss March, come to my desk," he roared, "and bring your limes with you!"

Amy left six behind and took the rest to him.

"Is that all?" he asked.

"Not quite," Amy answered.

"Bring the rest immediately!" Mr Davis shouted.

Amy obeyed.

"Now take these disgusting things two by two, and throw them out of the window," the teacher said.

Scarlet with shame and anger, Amy went backwards and forwards six dreadful times. As she returned from her last trip, Mr Davis stood up.

"Miss March, hold out your hand!" he said.

Amy, shocked, put both hands behind her back and stared at him.

"Your hand, Miss March!" he said again.

Too proud to beg, Amy gritted her teeth and held out her hand. Several blows made the palm of her hand tingle. She did not mind the pain. No, what hurt was this – for the first time in her life, she had been struck.

Amy was in a sad state when she arrived home for lunch. Mrs March did not say much. Meg bathed the injured hand with lotion and tears. Beth brought her kittens to comfort her. Jo suggested that Mr Davis should be arrested immediately.

Just before school closed that afternoon, Jo walked up to Mr Davis' desk and delivered a letter from her mother. Then she collected Amy's belongings.

"You were in the wrong, Amy," Mrs March said later that evening, "but I do not approve of hitting as a punishment. You can take a little vacation from school, and I want you to study every day with Beth. I shall ask your father's advice before I send you anywhere else."

"I wish all the girls would leave and spoil his school," Amy said.

"You broke the rules and you deserved to be punished," Mrs March said gently. "You are getting too conceited, Amy dear, and you must start to put it right."

Amy tried hard to be grown-up, but now and then she still acted like a spoilt child. One afternoon, Meg, Jo and Laurie went to see a show. Amy wanted to go too, but Jo had not bought a ticket for her. They left Amy shouting over the banister, "You'll be sorry for this, Jo March!"

When they came home, Amy was reading quietly. Jo decided that Amy had forgiven her. But she was mistaken. The next day, Jo burst into the room where Meg, Amy and Beth were reading.

"Has anyone taken my book?" she shouted.

Jo's book was her pride and joy. It was a half-dozen fairy tales that she had written for her father.

Meg and Beth said "No" at once. Amy poked the fire and said nothing. Jo saw her face turn red.

"Amy, you've got it!" she said.

"No, I haven't!"

"That's a lie!" Joe shouted, taking her by the shoulders and looking very fierce.

"You'll never see your silly old book again," Amy cried.

"Why not?"

"I burnt it."

Jo turned very pale, then she shook Amy until her teeth chattered in her head.

"You wicked, wicked girl!" she cried. "I can never write it again and I'll never forgive you as long as I live."

No one spoke of this great trouble, not even Mrs March. She knew it was better to wait until something softened Jo's anger. And this is what happened.

The next day, Laurie and Jo decided to go skating on

the river. Amy ran after them. As Jo set off across the ice she knew that Amy was putting on her skates at the edge of the river; but she did not turn round.

"Keep to the edge, it isn't safe in the middle!" Laurie shouted to Jo.

Jo heard. Amy did not.

"Let her take care of herself," Jo muttered to herself.

Jo started to skate after Laurie, but a strange feeling made her stop and turn round, just in time to see Amy throw up her hands as she fell through the ice. Her cry made Jo's heart stand still with fear. Then Laurie skated swiftly past her and together they dragged Amy out.

"I let her go into the middle of the ice," Jo wept to her mother when Amy was safe and warm in bed. "It's my dreadful temper. I went to bed angry, without forgiving Amy, and if it hadn't been for Laurie, it might have been too late. How could I be so wicked?"

As if she heard, Amy opened her eyes and held out her arms with a smile. Neither sister spoke, but they hugged each other.

And everything was forgiven and forgotten in a kiss.

CHAPTER FOUR
Meg is vain

One fine April day, Meg was on top of the world.

"I can't go to work because my pupils have got measles," she laughed, "and Annie Moffat, has invited me to stay."

The Moffats were very fashionable and Meg was unsure of herself. The house was so splendid and the people so elegant. But it was pleasant to ride in a fine carriage every day, and do nothing except have fun. Soon, she began to imitate her friends. The more she saw of Annie Moffat's pretty things, the more she envied her and wanted to be rich.

"Home seems so poor and shabby," she thought sadly.

One evening, the night of a small party, Meg took out her only party dress. It looked limper and older than ever. Meg saw the girls glance at it, then at one another. Meg's cheeks turned red. No one said a word, but Meg saw that they pitied her. Then the maid brought in a box of flowers. Annie ripped off the lid, gasping at the lovely roses inside.

"They are for Miss March," the maid said, holding out a note to her.

The girls giggled.

"Who are they from?"

"The note is from mother, and the flowers are from Laurie," Meg said simply.

The flowers cheered her up. She took some for herself, then she made up small bouquets for her friends. Meg enjoyed herself very much that evening, until she overheard a conversation. One voice asked,

"How old is she?"

"About sixteen or seventeen," the other voice replied.

"Poor thing! She'd be so pretty if she were in fashion. Do you think she'd be offended if we offered to lend her a dress for the party on Thursday? They say Mrs March is hoping that one of her daughters will marry the Laurence boy. I shall invite him on Thursday."

Meg was angry. She tried to forget what she had heard; but she could not. How dare they say that about her mother! She was glad when the evening was over, and she cooled her hot cheeks with her tears before she went to sleep. Those foolish words had spoiled her happy and innocent world.

The afternoon of the big party, one of her friends asked, "What are you going to wear, Meg?"

"My old white dress again," she replied.

"I've got a sweet blue silk dress that I've outgrown," Belle said. "Will you wear it to please me?"

"Thank you, but I don't mind my old dress," Meg said.

"Please!" Belle said. "You'd be a little beauty with the right dress and hair."

Meg did not refuse again. She wanted to see how beautiful she could look! Belle and her maid laced Meg into a dress so tight that she could not breathe – and so low that she blushed when she saw herself in the mirror. They gave her earrings, bracelets and a necklace. They handed her blue silk boots, a lace handkerchief, a feathery fan and a bouquet of flowers.

When Meg went downstairs, she noticed that the other young people took her more seriously. Several young men asked to be introduced to her. Meg began to enjoy herself. Suddenly, as she flirted, she saw Laurie. He was staring at her in surprise. He bowed, smiled and said, "Jo wanted me to come and tell her how you looked."

"What shall you tell her?" Meg asked.

"I shall say I didn't know you," he said seriously.

"Don't you like the way I look?" Meg asked.

"No, I don't," was Laurie's blunt reply.

"You are the rudest boy I ever saw!" Meg exclaimed.

She left Laurie and went to stand by the window. As she cooled her hot cheeks against the glass, a friend of the Moffats went by with his mother.

"They are making a fool of that March girl," he said. "I wanted you to meet her. She was so fresh and charming before. But she looks like a doll tonight."

"Oh dear," Meg sighed. "Why wasn't I more sensible? I am so ashamed of myself."

She begged Laurie not to tell her family. But when Meg returned home, she told her mother all about her silliness.

"Don't worry, Meg," her mother smiled. "You have no reason to be ashamed because you are poor. And being poor will not put off a man who really loves you."

CHAPTER FIVE
Lazy days

It was the first day of June, and Meg and Jo were in very high spirits.

"I have three whole months' holiday!" Meg laughed as she came home.

"And Aunt March left for the seaside today!" Jo cried. "I thought she was going to make me go with her right until the last minute."

"What are you going to do with your holiday?" Amy asked.

"Stay in bed late and do only what I want," Meg said at once.

"I'm going to sit up in the apple-tree and read all day," Jo said.

Amy turned to Beth. "Don't let us have any lessons, then," she said. 'We'll play all the time like the others."

"May we do whatever we want, mother?" Meg asked Mrs March.

"You may try your experiment for a week, and see how you like it," she told them.

They began the experiment by being lazy for the rest of that day. The next morning, Meg did not get up until ten o'clock. She had breakfast alone. It did not taste very good because the room seemed lonely and untidy. Jo had not brought in any fresh flowers, Beth had not dusted and Amy's books lay everywhere. Only their mother's corner was neat and tidy.

As the days passed the girls felt more and more restless. By Friday night, they were all sick of the experiment, although nobody would admit it. But Mrs March decided to really teach them what no work meant. On Saturday, she gave Hannah the day off.

When the girls came downstairs on Saturday morning, there was no fire in the kitchen and no breakfast in the dining room.

"It has been a hard week for me," Mrs March called from her room, "you must do the best you can today. I'm going to rest. Then I'm going out to lunch."

"Oh," said Jo, "I'm aching to do something different. I'll cook the midday meal. I'll invite Laurie!"

"Don't try too many new dishes," Meg warned her.

"Everything seems out of sorts today," Jo muttered to herself, "and now I can hear Beth crying. That's a sure sign that something's wrong in the family."

Jo hurried into the parlour to find Beth sobbing over Pip, the canary. He lay dead in the cage, with his little claws stretched out as if he were begging for food.

"It's all my fault!" Beth wept. "I forgot him − there isn't a seed left to eat or a drop of water to drink. O Pip!

How could I be so cruel to you?"

"Lay him in a box," Jo said, "and after lunch, we'll have a nice little funeral."

Jo went into the kitchen, put on an apron and started work. She discovered that the fire that heated the oven had gone out. She re-lit it. Then she went shopping while it heated again. Jo was pleased with herself as she trudged home with her shopping. She had bought some good bargains – a very small lobster, some very old asparagus and two boxes of cheap strawberries.

The meal that Jo served up that day became a family joke. She did not ask for any advice, but did her best alone. She boiled the asparagus for an hour, but found the stalks were harder than ever. She hammered and poked at the lobster until its shell came off and she realised there would not be enough for them all. The bread burnt black and the strawberries were not as ripe as they looked.

Half an hour later than usual, a hot and tired Jo rang the bell for lunch. Poor Jo! She wanted to hide under the table as the others tasted one thing after another, then pushed the food to the side of their plates. Laurie talked and laughed to cheer them all up.

"At least the strawberries will taste all right," Jo thought, as she put them on the table. "I've sugared them well and there's a jug of cream to go with them."

Amy took a spoonful and choked.

"What's wrong?" Jo asked, trembling.

"Salt instead of sugar and the cream is sour," said Meg.

Jo groaned and turned red. She was just about to cry when her eyes met Laurie's. Suddenly, she saw the funny side and started to laugh until the tears ran down her cheeks. So did everybody else and the meal ended happily with bread and butter and laughter.

Soon they became serious again for Beth's sake. Laurie dug a little grave in the garden and Beth laid Pip in it.

As darkness fell that evening, the family gathered on the porch. Each girl groaned as she sat down.

"What a dreadful day this has been!" Jo said.

When Mrs March came home, she asked brightly: "Have you enjoyed your experiment, girls? Do you want to carry on for another week?"

"No!" her daughters cried together.

Mrs March smiled. "I thought it was time to show you what happens when everyone thinks only of herself. And now, when you start your little jobs again, you will know that they are good for you. Work gives you independence and power, much more than money or the latest fashion."

"We'll remember, mother!" they said together.

And they did.

CHAPTER SIX
Day dreams

One warm September afternoon, Laurie swung to and fro in his hammock. He was in a bad mood. He had done very little studying that day and his tutor, Mr Brooke, was angry with him. He stared up into the green gloom of the horse-chestnut trees above him. Suddenly, he heard voices. Peeping down, he saw the March girls leaving their house. Where were they going?

Each one of them wore a large, floppy hat and carried a bag. Meg had a cushion, Jo a book, Beth a basket and Amy a drawing pad. All walked quietly through the garden, out at the little back gate. Then they began to climb the hill that rose between the house and the river.

"Well, that's unkind!" Laurie said to himself, "to have a picnic and not ask me. I'll see what's going on!"

Laurie found the girls under a clump of pine trees on the hill. He stood watching them from a distance until Beth waved him over.

"May I join you, please, or shall I be a nuisance?" he asked, slowly walking towards them.

Meg lifted her eyebrows, but Jo looked crossly at her.

"Of course you may," Jo said. "Finish reading this story to us." Laurie did as she asked.

"What do you dream of doing?" Jo asked him as he closed the book.

"After I've travelled the world, I'd like to live abroad and have as much music as I choose," he replied. "I want to be a famous musician. What do you dream of, Meg?"

"I shall be mistress of my own house. It will be full of beautiful things. I shall do good works and make everyone love me," she said.

"Would you like a master for your house?" Laurie asked.

"You know it wouldn't be perfect for you without a good husband and some little children!" Jo said bluntly. "Why don't you say so?"

"You'll have nothing but horses and novels in yours," Meg laughed.

"And I'd write out of a magic inkpot so that my

novels will be as famous as Laurie's music," Jo said. "I intend to astonish you all one day. Yes, I think I shall write books and be rich and famous."

"My dream is to stay at home safe with father and mother, and take care of the family," Beth said happily.

"I have so many wishes," Amy said, "but my favourite is to go to Rome and paint. I want to be the best artist in the world."

"I wonder if any of us will get our wishes," Laurie said, chewing grass like a cow.

"If we are all alive ten years from now, let us see how many of us have got our wishes, or how much nearer we are to them," Jo said.

"I shall be twenty-seven!" Meg exclaimed.

"You and I will be twenty-six, Laurie," Jo laughed, "Beth twenty-four and Amy twenty-two."

"I'm afraid I shall be too lazy to do what I plan," Laurie cried, suddenly jumping to his feet.

"Mother says you need a motive," Jo told him, "and then you will work very hard."

"I will, if only I get the chance!" Laurie cried excitedly. "I know I ought to please my grandfather and do what he wants. But I really want to break away, like my father did, and I would tomorrow if there was anyone else to stay with my grandfather."

"You should sail away and never come home again

until you have tried your own way," Jo said.

"That's not right, Jo," Meg interrupted, "and Laurie must not take your bad advice. There is no one else to stay and love Mr Laurence. Do your duty and you'll get your reward. That is what Mr Brooke has done. Everyone respects and loves him."

"And what do you know about my tutor?" Laurie asked, smiling.

"I know that he took care of his own mother until she died," Meg replied. "And that he is a kind man."

"Yes, he's a dear old fellow!" Laurie said.

"And you can start doing your duty by working hard for Mr Brooke," Meg said, blushing.

Rather objecting to this lecture, Laurie replied mischievously, "I see he bows and smiles when he passes your window."

Meg put out her hand, fondly and timidly.

"Please do not be hurt, Laurie," she said, "you are like a brother to me. Forgive me. I meant to be kind."

Ashamed of his mischief-making, Laurie shook Meg's hand. Then he made himself as helpful as possible, until the sound of the tea bell reached them. That night, when Beth played the piano for his grandfather, Laurie stood in the shadows, listening.

"I'll let my dreams go," he thought, "and stay with the dear old man as long as he needs me. I am all that he has."

CHAPTER SEVEN

Secrets

The October days were growing cold and the sun shone for only a few hours each day through the high window of the attic where Jo sat on an old sofa, writing busily. One day, the last page was filled.

"There! I've done my best!" Jo exclaimed, as she threw down her pen.

She rolled up the sheets of paper, tied them up with a red ribbon and crept downstairs. She put on her hat and jacket as quietly as possible, climbed out on to the roof of the porch and swung herself down on to the grassy bank at the side of the house. Then she set off for town.

Jo found the place she was looking for and stood outside for a moment. At last, she went inside the building and came out ten minutes later, very red in the face. She found Laurie waiting for her, peering at one of the signs on the door. It said DENTIST.

"How many did you have out?" he asked.

Jo laughed.

"What are you up to?" Laurie asked.

"What are you doing here?" Jo asked. "I saw you come out of that billiard hall over there. I didn't think you went to such places."

"I don't. I was taking a fencing lesson," Laurie replied.

"I'm glad," Jo told him.

"Do you worry about me, Jo?" Laurie asked.

"A little," she replied, "You've got such a strong will, that I'm afraid that if you started to go wrong, it would be hard to stop you."

"Are you going to lecture me all the way home?" Laurie said. "I have got something interesting to tell you if you'll listen. But if I tell you my secret, you must tell me yours."

"Well," Jo said, "I've just left two stories with a newspaper. I'll hear next week whether they'll be printed or not."

Laurie threw his hat into the air and caught it.

"Hurrah for Miss March!" he shouted, "the famous American writer!"

Jo's eyes sparkled, for it is always pleasant when other people believe in you.

"What's your secret, Laurie?" she asked.

"I know where Meg's glove is. You remember, the one she lost during the summer?"

"Is that all?" Jo asked, disappointed.

"It's quite enough when I tell you where it is," Laurie said. He bent down and whispered three words in Jo's ear. She stood and stared at him for a moment, looking both surprised and unhappy. Then she walked on, saying sharply, "How do you know?"

"Saw it."

"Where?"

"Pocket," Laurie said. "Isn't it romantic?"

"No," Jo said. "It's horrid. I'm disgusted."

"I thought you would be pleased." Laurie said.

"At the idea of a somebody taking Meg away from us?" Jo said angrily.

"Race down this hill with me and you'll feel better," Laurie said.

Jo hesitated, but no one was in sight. She ran off, losing her hat and scattering hair pins as she ran. Laurie was right. She arrived at the bottom of the hill with bright eyes, glowing cheeks and no sign of anger on her face. Jo hoped nobody would pass by until she was tidy again. But someone did. It was Meg.

"You've been running, Jo!" she cried. "How could you! When will you stop such behaviour?"

"Not until I'm stiff and old and have to use crutches," Jo shouted. "Don't make me try to grow up before my time, Meg. It's hard enough to have you change all of a sudden. Let me be a little girl as long as I can."

For the next week or two, Jo behaved strangely. She was rude to Mr Brooke whenever they met. She often stared at Meg before suddenly jumping up to kiss her. On the second Saturday, Jo ran into the parlour and threw herself on to the sofa to read a newspaper.

"Have you anything interesting there?" Meg asked.

"Only a story," Jo said.

"Read it out aloud," Amy said.

Jo began to read very fast.

"Who wrote it?" Beth asked at the end.

Jo suddenly sat up straight, threw down the paper and announced in a loud voice, "Your sister!"

"You?" Meg cried, dropping her sewing.

"It's very good," Amy said.

"I knew it! I knew it!" Beth said, hugging her sister. "Oh, my Jo, I'm so proud!"

Jo wept a few happy tears. To win the praise of those she loved seemed the happiest thing of all.

CHAPTER EIGHT

Mrs March goes away

"November is the most horrible month in the whole year," Meg complained, standing at the window one dull afternoon.

"That's the reason I was born in it," Jo said.

"If something pleasant happened, we should think it was a delightful month," Beth said.

"Nothing pleasant ever happens in November," Meg said. "We trudge on day after day, never having any fun."

"Two pleasant things are going to happen right away," Beth replied. "Mother is walking down the path and Laurie is on his way through the garden."

Soon after they had both arrived, the doorbell rang. Hannah came in, holding an envelope. Mrs March read the two lines it contained and dropped back into her chair as if the paper had sent a bullet through her heart. Jo read out aloud in a frightened voice:

Mrs March:
Your husband is very ill. Come at once.
S. Hale,
Union Hospital, Washington.

How still the room was! How dark the day became! How suddenly the whole world seemed to change!

"I shall go at once," Mrs March cried, "but it may be too late! Oh, children, help me to bear it!"

For several minutes there was nothing but the sound of sobbing in the room. Then Mrs March got up.

"There's no more time for tears now," she said quickly. "Be calm now, girls, and let me think. Laurie, send a telegram to say I will come at once. The next train leaves early in the morning. I can take that. Then take this note to Aunt March, for I must borrow money to pay the fare."

A few minutes later, Laurie rode past their window.

"Beth, go and ask Mr Laurence for two bottles of old wine. I'm not too proud to beg for your father. Amy, get out the black trunk. Meg, come and help me pack."

As Meg crossed the hall, she met Mr Brooke.

"I am very sorry to hear of this, Miss March," he said quietly. "I have come to offer to go with your mother to Washington."

"How kind you are!" Meg cried. "Mother will accept, I'm sure. Thank you very much!"

Jo was nowhere to be seen as the afternoon passed by. Eventually everybody was so worried that Laurie went off to look for her. While he was away, Jo came in, and put twenty-five dollar notes on the table.

"That's for you, mother, to buy anything that father needs!" she said.

"My dear, where did you get it?" her mother cried. "I hope you haven't done anything silly."

"No, it's mine," Jo told her. "I only sold what was mine."

As she spoke, Jo took off her bonnet. Her long thick hair was cut short. "Your hair! Your beautiful hair! Your one beauty!" they all cried. But Beth hugged Jo's cropped head.

The next morning, Mrs March left, accompanied by Mr Brooke.

CHAPTER NINE
Dark days

Ten days after Mrs March's departure, Beth went to visit a poor family nearby – the same family who had eaten their breakfast the Christmas before. Everybody else was too busy. But when Beth came back home, Jo found her upstairs, crying.

"You've had scarlet fever, haven't you?" Beth asked.

"Yes, years ago, when Meg did," Jo replied. "Why?"

"Oh, Jo, the baby's dead! From scarlet fever!"

"If only mother were at home," Jo cried.

"Don't let Amy come in," Beth said. "She didn't have it. And neither did I."

Amy was sent to stay with Aunt March and, a few days later, Beth fell ill with scarlet fever. She was much sicker than anybody expected.

"We must not tell mother," Jo said to Meg. "Not yet."

But Beth became slowly and steadily worse.

How dark the house seemed! How heavy were the hearts of the sisters as they waited while the shadow of death hovered over the once happy home! The first of December was a wintry day. A bitter wind blew, snow fell fast and the year seemed to be getting ready to end. When the doctor arrived that morning, he held Beth's hot hand and whispered to Hannah, "If Mrs March can leave her husband, you'd better send for her."

Jo rushed out into the storm to send a telegram. She was soon back, just as Laurie came in with a letter bearing the glad news that Mr March was improving. Laurie looked very pleased with himself.

"What is it?" Jo asked, forgetting her unhappiness for a moment.

"I telegraphed your mother yesterday," Laurie said, his face red with excitement. "She'll be here tonight, on the late train. I'll fetch her from the station. Then everything will be all right. Aren't you glad I did it?"

Jo turned very pale and threw her arms around his neck, crying, "Oh, Laurie! Oh, mother! I am so glad!" Laurie patted her gently. Suddenly, he kissed her. Jo pushed him away, "No, don't!"

Now a breath of fresh air seemed to blow through the house. Every time the girls met, their pale faces broke into smiles and they hugged one another, whispering, "Mother's coming!" But Beth still lay unconscious.

"There should be a change for the better – or the worse – about midnight," the doctor warned them.

The girls never forgot that night. They did not sleep as they kept watch over Beth. The house was as still as death. Nothing was heard except the wailing of the wind. It was past two when Jo went to stand by the

window. Suddenly, she saw Meg kneeling by her mother's chair, her face hidden. "Beth is dead," Jo whispered, "and Meg is afraid to tell me."

Jo rushed to Beth's bedside. A change seemed to have taken place. The look of pain and fever had left her face. She looked peaceful. Jo leaned over, kissed Beth's damp forehead and whispered, "Goodbye, my Beth, goodbye!"

As Jo spoke, Hannah stirred. She looked at Beth, felt her face and hands and cried, "The fever's broken! Praise the Lord!" Soon after, the doctor arrived.

"Yes, she will pull through," he told them.

Never had the world seemed so lovely to Meg and Jo that morning. Then they heard Laurie's voice saying, in a happy whisper, "Girls! She's home! She's home!"

I don't think I have any words in which to tell the meeting of the mother and daughters. Such times are beautiful to live, but very hard to describe. So I will only say that the house was full of happiness. That evening, while Meg was writing to her father, Jo went to her mother and stood there, twisting her fingers in her hair.

"What is it, dear?" her mother asked.

"I want to tell you something, mother," Jo said.

"About Meg?" her mother asked.

"How quickly you guessed!" Jo replied. "Mr Brooke has kept Meg's glove. Now isn't that dreadful?"

"John, Mr Brooke is an excellent young man," her mother replied. "Your father and I have become very fond of him. He has told us that he loves Meg. Don't say anything to her, Jo, not yet. She is too young to marry. Meg does not love John yet, but she will soon learn to."

CHAPTER TEN

A surprise Christmas present

Like sunshine after storm, the weeks that followed were peaceful. Beth was soon able to lie on the sofa all day, amusing herself with her cats and her doll's sewing. As Christmas Day came closer, an air of mystery began to haunt the house.

The day itself was unusually fine and Beth felt well enough for Laurie and Jo to carry her to the window to see their surprise – a snow maiden, crowned with holly and carrying a roll of sheet music in her hand.

"I'm so full of happiness," Beth whispered. "If father were here, I wouldn't be able to hold one drop more."

Half an hour later, Laurie opened the parlour door, his face full of excitement.

"Here's another Christmas present for the March family," he announced in a strange and breathless voice. He stepped back and in his place stood a tall man, leaning on the arm of Mr Brooke. Everybody in the room ran forward. Jo almost fainted. Mr Brooke kissed Meg by mistake. Amy tumbled over a stool and didn't get up, but lay there kissing her father's boots.

"Ssh, remember Beth! She's resting!" Mrs March whispered. But it was too late. The study door flew open

and Beth ran straight into her father's arms.

There was never such a Christmas dinner as they had that day. As darkness fell, the happy family gathered together around the fire. "Just a year ago we were grumbling about the terrible Christmas we were having," Jo said.

"It has been a rough road for my little women," Mr March said, "but you have all been very brave."

Mr March smiled and took hold of Meg's hand.

"I remember when this used to be smooth and white," he said, "but it is much prettier now with all its blisters and blemishes."

"What about Jo?" Beth whispered in his ear. "Say something nice because she has tried so hard."

"In spite of the curly short hair, I don't see the boyish Jo I left behind," Mr March smiled. "I see a young lady whose face is gentler, who is strong and helpful."

"Now Beth," Amy said, longing for her turn, but ready to wait.

"There's so little of her, I'm afraid to say much, for fear she will slip away altogether," their father began cheerfully. "But she is not as shy as she used to be."

Then he stroked Amy's shining hair. "You do not look at yourself in the mirror so much," he said. "I can see that you have learned to think of other people more than yourself."

"It's singing time now," Beth said, "and I want to play my piano again."

And as she played, she sang in the sweet voice they never thought they would hear again. Jo's eyes slowly glanced around the room.

"Everybody looks so happy now," she thought, "that I do not think the future could be any better than this."

Mrs March was right about Meg. She did learn to love John Brooke and they became engaged just before the end of this story. Jo never went back to work for Aunt March. Do you remember that Amy had to go and stay there when Beth had scarlet fever? Aunt March liked Amy so much that she bribed her with drawing lessons to work for her! At last, Jo was free to write. As well as starting her novel, she earned a dollar for each article published in one of the town's newspapers. As for Beth, she was never quite the rosy, healthy girl she had been. But she was happy, and always everyone's friend.